Library of Congress Cataloging-in-Publication Information available.
ISBN 978-1-951412-33-3
LCCN 2021902196

Manufactured in China.

10 9 8 7 6 5 4 3 2 1

The Collective Book Studio
Oakland, California
www.thecollectivebook.studio

THE
collective
BOOK STUDIO

For Neko
Y.P.

For Sofia
R.S.

LITTLE LOON
FINDS *his* VOICE

story by **YVONNE PEARSON**
pictures by **REGINA SHKLOVSKY**

THE
collective
BOOK STUDIO

Little Loon opened his bill.
Out came a whisper of a squeak.

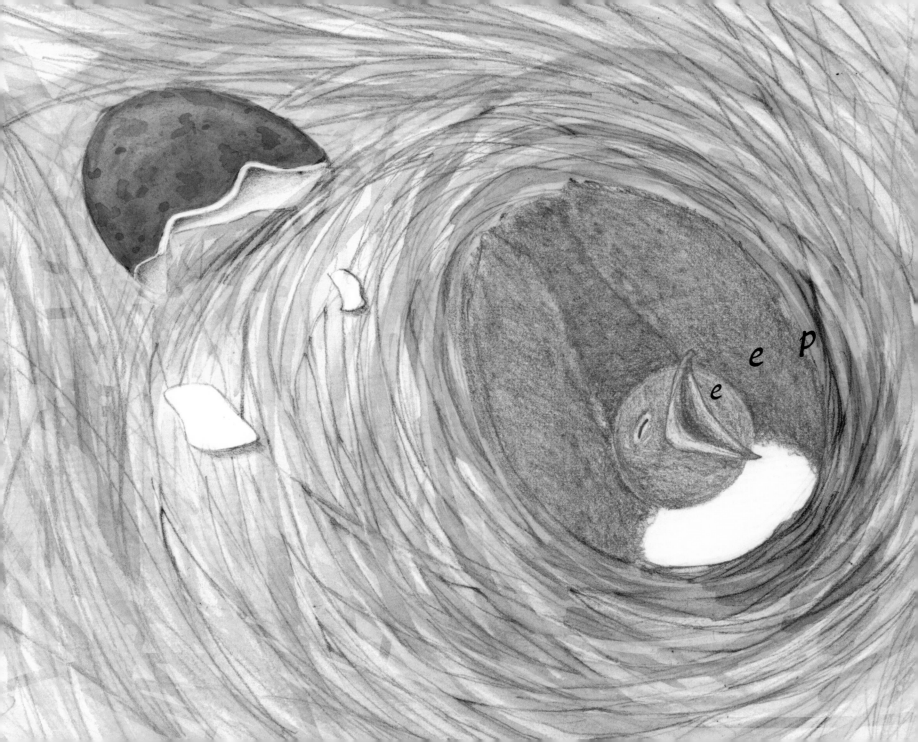

He couldn't wait to be bold and have a fearless call
like his Papa's.

hello

Ahhh oooo

Papa's wail arced above the trees,
soared through misty air, and rang off the rocks.
Papa's call was long. His call was strong.
It echoed on the water.

Little Loon rode Mama's back, slipping off when she dove.

Mama got the fish,
and Little Loon had lunch.

Each day Little Loon practiced his call.

e   e   P   e

One afternoon, a raven ventured toward their nest.
From Papa came a tremolo, a fluttering, pulsing sound
like lightning on the water.

Wo Hoo H Ho

DANGER WATCH

o Hoo Hoo Hoo
Hoo Hoo Hoo

Papa's call was long. His call was strong.
It echoed on the water.

Little Loon yearned to be as bold
and call as long as Papa.

He tried . . .

e
e
p

p e e p

s q u e a k

and he tried.

In the evening, Little Loon and
Mama explored behind tufts of grass.
Hoot, Papa blew, and *hoot* again.
Where are you?

Little Loon tried to answer.

It was even hard for him to hoot.
Mama answered, *Hoot! Here we are!*

Every day Little Loon opened
his bill for the dragonflies Papa
brought and practiced his *peeps*.

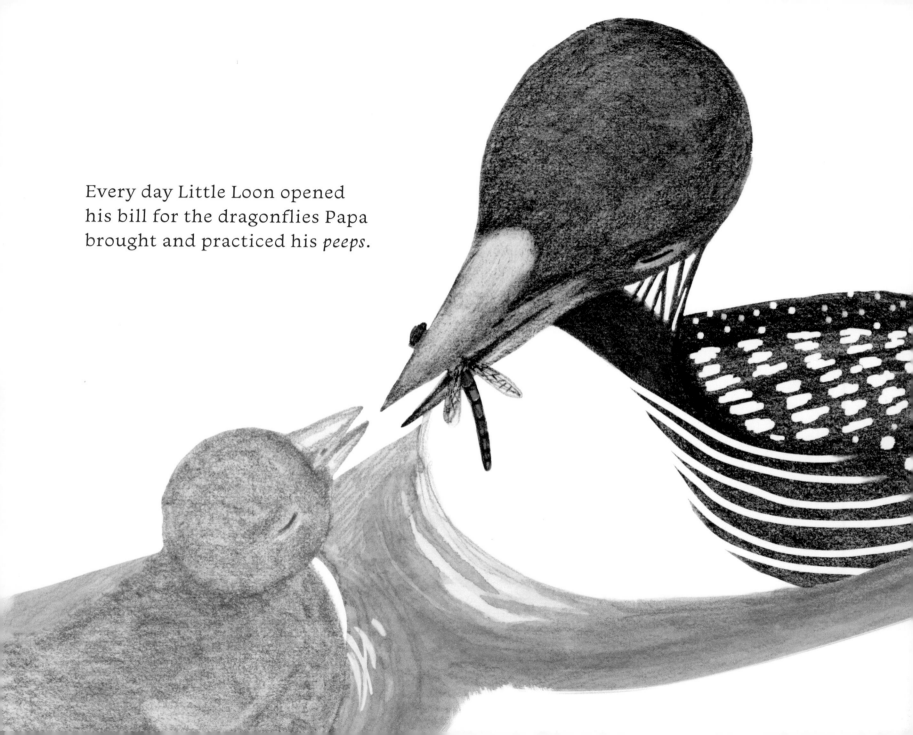

He opened his bill for the fish Mama brought and pushed out *squeaks*.

And each day he practiced some more.

He practiced while the fish grew bigger, the water warmer. Yellow lilies blossomed on the lake.

One day a new loon, a stranger, circled high above them, looking for a lake to claim.

Papa opened his bill and fluted a sharp yodel.

Papa's call was long.
His call was strong.
It echoed on the water.

Little Loon opened his bill
to make his own sharp call.

Ooo Woo Oo Ah Ah

Little Loon hung his head.

He floated in circles, listless through the days, and made no *peeps*, no *squeaks*. No *eeps* or *ooos* or *ahs*.

One morning, the sun grew
suddenly dark.

Little Loon looked about for Mama
and Papa, who were nowhere to be
found. They were fishing, diving
deep under the water.

A bird—bald and fierce and BIG—plunged
like a lightning bolt toward Little Loon.

Ah Oooooooooooooo

wailed Little Loon.

He was growing a bigger voice!
Papa's sharp yodel soon joined Little Loon's call,
and the eagle soared off.

Little Loon, filled with joy,
began to practice again.

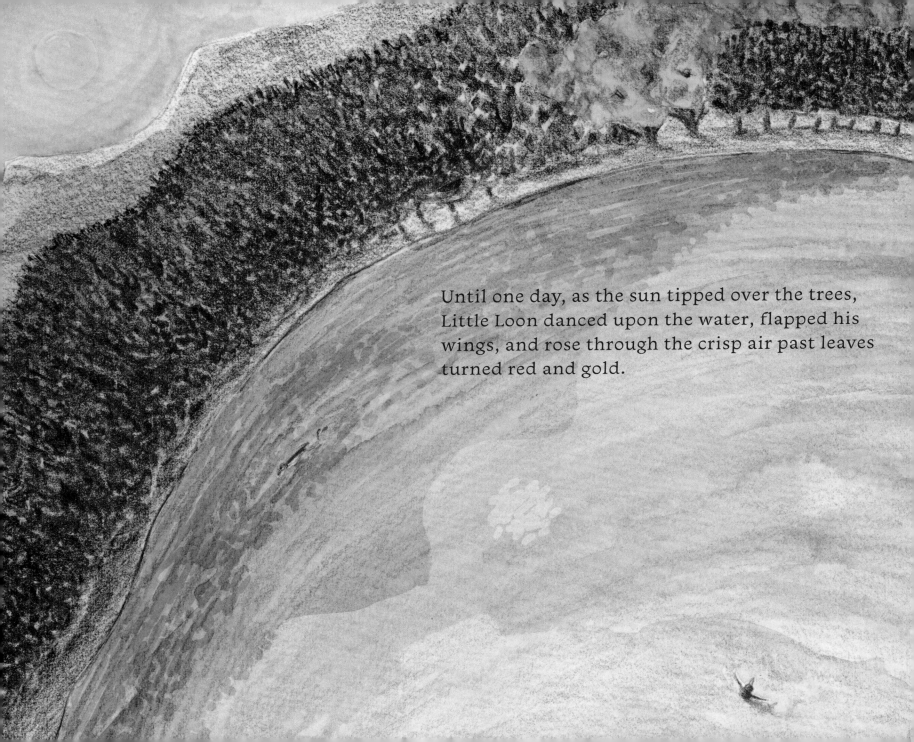

Until one day, as the sun tipped over the trees, Little Loon danced upon the water, flapped his wings, and rose through the crisp air past leaves turned red and gold.

His call was long. His call was strong.
It echoed on the water.

A Little More About Loons

Loon Calls

Common loons live in the United States, Canada, Iceland, and Greenland. They are found in Alaska, Idaho, Maine, Michigan, Minnesota, Montana, New Hampshire, New York, North Dakota, Vermont, Washington, and Wisconsin. In the winter they migrate to the Pacific and Atlantic coasts.

Loons are well known for the haunting sounds they make. They have four calls:

The **TREMOLO** is used to signal alarm. It is also called a "crazy laugh." The call is a trembling or quivering sound. The tremolo is the only call they make while they are flying.

The **WAIL** is a sort of howl, and it is used for social interaction among loons. "Hi, here I am. How are you?"

The **HOOT** is one short sound, almost like a big breath, that family members use to stay in contact.

The **YODEL** is a call made only by males used to defend territory. It is long and rising and can last up to six seconds. That may not seem like a long time, but if you try humming while you count slowly to six, you can see that it is a very long time for a bird's call. Each male loon's yodel is unique.

Chicks don't get their full adult voice until they are eight months old. They cannot yodel until they are about two years old.

Other Loon Facts

Common loons grow from two to three feet long. They look funny on land. They waddle comically because their feet are very far back on their bodies. They are more at home on the water.

In the spring the male and female loon build a nest together on the edge of forested lakes. They use moss, mud, pine needles, leaves, and other plants for the nest. The female lays one or two eggs and the male and female take turns incubating the eggs.

When the baby loons are born, they may ride on their parents' backs for a few days to stay safe from predators. Loons can swim and dive two or three days after they are born, but they cannot fly until they are about twelve weeks old. Then the young loons are ready to be independent from their parents.

Eagles are a common threat to loon chicks. When an eagle threatens, the chicks may swim to shore while the parents dive and swim away to divert the eagle. The chicks may also wail frantically and, if male, yodel as well. Eagles are not easy to drive off.

The common loon is not an endangered species. Still, global warming threatens them. The Audubon Society estimates that their summer range will be reduced by 56 percent and their winter range by 75 percent within sixty years.

You can hear a loon's call at www.loon.org.

Yvonne Pearson has written more than a dozen children's books, and her poetry has appeared in numerous publications. She is a 2018 McKnight Writing Fellow and has received two Minnesota State Arts Board grants as well as the Creative Non-Fiction Award and the Shabo Award in children's literature from the Loft Literary Center. She has three grown children and three grandchildren, and lives with her husband in Minneapolis, Minnesota.

Regina Shklovsky is an illustrator and graphic designer based in Sonoma County, California. She received a 2018 Nautilus Award and a 2019 Moonbeam Award for her children's book, *Fun in the Mud: A Wetlands Tale*. Her work has also been featured on the Illustrator's Wall for the Bologna Children's Book Fair. When time permits, you will most likely find her adventuring in nature with her husband and daughter.